Introduction

Welcome to the book "Fundamentals of HTML, CSS, and JavaScript Programming!" This book aims to help you get started in the exciting world of web development by exploring the fundamental technologies of HTML, CSS, and JavaScript.

With HTML, you can structure your web pages in an organized manner, while CSS allows you to add style and design. JavaScript brings dynamism and interactivity to your projects. In the introductory chapter, we will briefly overview these technologies, understanding how they work together in modern web development.

Throughout the book, interactive examples will guide you, allowing you to apply what you've learned in practice. Whether you are creating a simple webpage or a more complex application, this book will smoothly guide you into the realm of web development!

Table of Contents

We hope this book will guide you through the exploration of the HTML, CSS, and JavaScript world!

What is Web Development?

Web development refers to the process of creating and building websites or web applications that are accessible via the internet. It encompasses a wide range of activities, including designing the visual layout of a site, coding its functionality, and managing the server-side components to ensure proper functionality.

Key aspects of web development include:

1. Frontend Development:
   - Involves building the user interface and user experience that visitors interact with.
   - Utilizes technologies like HTML for structure, CSS for styling, and JavaScript for interactivity.
2. Backend Development:
   - Focuses on the server-side of the application, dealing with databases, server logic, and ensuring data is processed and stored correctly.
   - Common backend languages include Python, Ruby, PHP, and Node.js.
3. Full-stack Development:
   - Encompasses both frontend and backend development, allowing developers to work on all aspects of a web application.
4. Web Design:
   - Includes the visual aspects of a website, such as layout, color schemes, and typography, contributing to a positive user experience.
5. Web Accessibility:
   - Ensures that websites are inclusive and can be used by people with disabilities. This involves designing and coding with accessibility standards in mind.
6. Web Security:
   - Involves implementing measures to protect websites and web applications from potential security threats, such as data breaches and unauthorized access.
7. Responsive Design:

- Ensures that websites work well on various devices and screen sizes, adapting to different resolutions and orientations.

Web development is a dynamic field that continuously evolves with advancements in technologies and standards. Professionals in this field collaborate across disciplines to create effective, secure, and visually appealing online experiences.

Role of HTML, CSS, and JavaScript

The role of HTML, CSS, and JavaScript is fundamental in the realm of web development, each serving a specific purpose to create dynamic and interactive websites.

1. HTML (Hypertext Markup Language):
   - Purpose: HTML is the backbone of web development, providing the structural foundation for web pages. It defines the elements on a page, such as headings, paragraphs, images, and links.
   - Role: HTML organizes content, making it readable for browsers. It establishes the hierarchy and structure of information, forming the skeleton of a webpage.
2. CSS (Cascading Style Sheets):
   - Purpose: CSS focuses on the presentation and styling of web content. It enables developers to control the layout, colors, fonts, and overall visual aesthetics of a webpage.
   - Role: CSS enhances the user experience by ensuring consistency in design and layout. It separates the structure defined by HTML from the visual representation, allowing for easier maintenance and flexibility.
3. JavaScript:

- Purpose: JavaScript adds interactivity and dynamic behavior to web pages. It enables developers to create responsive and engaging user interfaces.
- Role: JavaScript allows for the manipulation of HTML and CSS in real-time, facilitating actions like form validation, animation, and asynchronous communication with servers. It turns static web pages into dynamic applications.

In summary, HTML provides the structure, CSS enhances the presentation, and JavaScript adds the interactivity to create a cohesive and user-friendly web experience. Together, these technologies form the core trio that powers modern web development, allowing developers to build a wide range of applications from static pages to complex, dynamic web solutions.

HTML Basics

Structure of an HTML Document

HTML (Hypertext Markup Language) serves as the foundation for creating web pages, and its structure is essential for organizing content. A typical HTML document is composed of several key elements:

1. Document Type Declaration (DOCTYPE):
   - Specifies the HTML version being used. It helps browsers interpret the document correctly.
2. html
3. Copy code
4. `<!DOCTYPE html>`
5. HTML Element:
   - Serves as the root element, encapsulating the entire content of the page.
   - Contains two main sections: `<head>` and `<body>`.

6. html

7. Copy code

8. `<html> <!-- Head and Body sections go here --> </html>`

9. Head Section:
   - Houses meta-information about the HTML document, such as the title, character set, linked stylesheets, and scripts.

10. html

11. Copy code

12. `<head> <title>Page Title</title> <!-- Other meta-information, styles, and scripts go here --> </head>`

13. Body Section:
   - Encloses the main content of the HTML document, encompassing text, images, links, and various other elements.

14. html

15. Copy code

16. `<body> <h1>This is a Heading</h1> <p>This is a paragraph.</p> <!-- Other content goes here --> </body>`

17. Heading Elements (h1 to h6):
   - Define different levels of headings, with `<h1>` as the highest level and `<h6>` as the lowest.

18. html

19. Copy code

20. `<h1>Main Heading</h1> <h2>Subheading</h2> <!-- ... --> <h6>Lowest Level Heading</h6>`

21. Paragraph Element:
   - Represents a block of text within the document.

22. html

23. Copy code

24. `<p>This is a paragraph of text.</p>`

25. Other Common Elements:
   - Include links (`<a>`), images (`<img>`), lists (`<ul>`, `<ol>`, `<li>`), and more, each contributing to the structured organization of content.

Understanding the hierarchical structure and purpose of these HTML elements is foundational for creating well-structured and semantically meaningful web pages.

HTML Elements and Tags

In HTML (Hypertext Markup Language), elements and tags are fundamental components used to structure and define content within a web page.

1. HTML Elements:
    - HTML documents consist of elements, which are the building blocks of content.
    - An element is typically composed of a start tag, content, and an end tag. For example:
    - html
    - Copy code
    - <p>This is a paragraph.</p>
2. HTML Tags:
    - Tags define the beginning and end of an HTML element. They are enclosed in angle brackets.
    - Start tags are written with the element name, and end tags have a forward slash before the element name.
    - html
    - Copy code
    - <p>Start tag</p>
3. Attributes:
    - HTML elements can have attributes, providing additional information about the element.
    - Attributes are always included in the start tag and consist of a name and a value.

- o html
- o Copy code
- o `<a href="https://www.example.com">Visit Example.com</a>`

4. Common HTML Elements:

- o `<p>`: Represents a paragraph of text.
- o `<a>`: Creates a hyperlink, linking to another resource.
- o `<img>`: Embeds an image in the document.
- o `<h1>`, `<h2>`, ... `<h6>`: Define headings of various levels.
- o `<ul>`, `<ol>`, `<li>`: Create unordered or ordered lists.

Basic HTML Attributes

HTML attributes provide additional information about elements and are always included in the start tag. Some common attributes include:

1. class:

- o Groups elements with similar styles, allowing for consistent styling across a website.
- o html
- o Copy code
- o `<p class="highlight">This paragraph has a special style.</p>`

2. id:

- o Uniquely identifies an element, often used for specific styling or JavaScript interactions.
- o html
- o Copy code
- o `<div id="header">Main Header</div>`

3. src:

- o Specifies the source URL for elements like images.

- o   html
- o   Copy code
- o   `<img src="image.jpg" alt="A descriptive text">`

4. `href`:

- o   Defines the hyperlink destination for anchor (<a>) elements.
- o   html
- o   Copy code
- o   `<a href="https://www.example.com">Visit Example.com</a>`

Understanding and utilizing HTML elements, tags, and attributes are crucial for effectively structuring content and creating dynamic and visually appealing web pages.

CSS Basics

CSS Syntax and Rules

CSS (Cascading Style Sheets) is a style language used to describe the presentation of HTML documents. Understanding its syntax and rules is essential for applying styles to elements on a web page.

CSS Syntax:

1. Selectors:

- o   Selectors target HTML elements to which styles will be applied.
- o   Examples:
- o   css
- o   Copy code
- o   `p { /* Styles for all paragraphs */ } .highlight { /* Styles for elements with class 'highlight' */ } #header { /* Styles for the element with id 'header' */ }`

2. **Declaration Block:**
   - Contains property-value pairs that define the styles for the selected elements.
   - Enclosed in curly braces {}.
   - css
   - Copy code

```css
p { color: blue; font-size: 16px; }
```

3. **Properties:**
   - Represent specific styling attributes like color, font-size, margin, etc.
   - Follow the selector and are separated from values by a colon.
   - css
   - Copy code

```css
p { color: blue; /* Property: color, Value: blue */ }
```

4. **Values:**
   - Specify the desired setting for a property.
   - Follow the property and are separated from other declarations by a semicolon.
   - css
   - Copy code

```css
p { color: blue; font-size: 16px; /* Values: blue, 16px */ }
```

5. **Comments:**
   - Enhance code readability but do not affect styles.
   - Enclosed in /* */.
   - css
   - Copy code

```css
/* This is a comment */
```

CSS Rules:

1. Specificity:

- Determines which style rule applies when multiple rules target the same element.
- More specific selectors take precedence.
- css
- Copy code
- /* Higher specificity */ #header { color: red; } /* Lower specificity */ .highlight { color: blue; }

2. Inheritance:
    - Some styles are inherited from parent elements to their children.
    - For example, the font property is often inherited.

Understanding the CSS syntax and rules empowers developers to create visually appealing and consistent designs across web pages.

CSS Styles and Formatting

In CSS (Cascading Style Sheets), styles and formatting play a crucial role in defining the appearance of HTML elements on a web page. Let's delve into the key aspects:

CSS Styles:

1. Color Property:
    - Specifies the text color or background color of an element.
    - css
    - Copy code
    - p { color: #333; /* Hexadecimal color code */ background-color: lightgray; }

2. Font Property:
    - Controls the font properties like family, size, weight, and style.
    - css
    - Copy code

- o body { font-family: 'Arial', sans-serif; /* Font family */ font-size: 16px; /* Font size */ font-weight: bold; /* Font weight */ font-style: italic; /* Font style */ }

3. Text Property:
   - o Manages text-related styles, including alignment, decoration, and spacing.
   - o css
   - o Copy code
   - o h1 { text-align: center; /* Text alignment */ text-decoration: underline; /* Underline text */ letter-spacing: 2px; /* Letter spacing */ }

CSS Formatting:

1. Box Model:
   - o Describes the layout of elements, including content, padding, border, and margin.
   - o css
   - o Copy code
   - o div { width: 200px; padding: 10px; border: 1px solid #999; margin: 20px; }

2. Positioning:
   - o Determines how elements are positioned on the page.
   - o css
   - o Copy code
   - o .absolute-position { position: absolute; top: 50px; left: 100px; } .relative-position { position: relative; top: 20px; left: 30px; }

3. Flexbox and Grid:
   - o Modern layout models for creating flexible and responsive designs.

- o   css
- o   Copy code
- o   `.flex-container { display: flex; justify-content: space-between; } .grid-container { display: grid; grid-template-columns: repeat(3, 1fr); }`

4. Media Queries:
   - o   Adapt styles based on the characteristics of the device or screen.
   - o   css
   - o   Copy code
   - o   `@media screen and (max-width: 600px) { body { font-size: 14px; } }`

CSS styles and formatting enable developers to craft visually appealing and responsive web designs, ensuring a positive user experience across various devices and screen sizes.

CSS Selectors and Classes

In CSS (Cascading Style Sheets), selectors and classes are fundamental concepts that allow developers to target specific HTML elements and apply styles efficiently. Let's explore these concepts in detail:

CSS Selectors:
1. Type Selector:
   - o   Selects all instances of a specific HTML element type.
   - o   css
   - o   Copy code
   - o   `p { /* Styles for all paragraphs */ }`
2. Class Selector:
   - o   Targets elements with a specific class attribute.

- o css
- o Copy code
- o `.highlight { /* Styles for elements with class 'highlight' */ }`

3. **ID Selector:**

   - o Selects a single element with a specific ID attribute.
   - o css
   - o Copy code
   - o `#header { /* Styles for the element with id 'header' */ }`

4. **Attribute Selector:**

   - o Selects elements based on the presence or value of their attributes.
   - o css
   - o Copy code
   - o `input[type="text"] { /* Styles for text input elements */ }`

5. **Descendant Selector:**

   - o Selects elements that are descendants of a specified element.
   - o css
   - o Copy code
   - o `article p { /* Styles for paragraphs within article elements */ }`

6. **Child Selector:**

   - o Selects elements that are direct children of a specified element.
   - o css
   - o Copy code
   - o `ul > li { /* Styles for list items that are direct children of a ul */ }`

CSS Classes:

1. **Defining a Class:**

   - o Classes are defined in the HTML using the `class` attribute.

- ○ html
- ○ Copy code
- ○ <p class="important-text">This text is important.</p>

2. Applying Styles with Classes:
   - ○ Styles associated with a class are defined in the CSS.
   - ○ css
   - ○ Copy code
   - ○ .important-text { font-weight: bold; color: red; }

3. Multiple Classes:
   - ○ An element can have multiple classes, allowing for the application of various styles.
   - ○ html
   - ○ Copy code
   - ○ <div class="box highlight-border"></div>
   - ○ css
   - ○ Copy code
   - ○ .box { width: 100px; height: 100px; } .highlight-border { border: 2px solid yellow; }

Understanding CSS selectors and classes provides developers with powerful tools to precisely target elements and create modular, reusable styles across their web projects.

JavaScript Basics

Variables and Data Types

JavaScript is a versatile programming language used for creating dynamic and interactive web pages. Understanding variables and data types is fundamental for effective JavaScript development.

1. Variables:
   - Variables are containers for storing data values.
   - Declared using the `var`, `let`, or `const` keyword.
   - javascript
   - Copy code

   ```javascript
   var myVariable; // Declaration myVariable = 10; // Assignment
   ```

2. Data Types:
   - JavaScript has dynamic typing, meaning variables can hold values of any data type.
   - Common data types include:
     - Number: Represents numeric values.
     - javascript
     - Copy code

       ```javascript
       var age = 25;
       ```
     - String: Represents textual data.
     - javascript
     - Copy code

       ```javascript
       var name = "John";
       ```
     - Boolean: Represents true or false values.
     - javascript
     - Copy code

       ```javascript
       var isStudent = true;
       ```
     - Array: Represents an ordered list of values.
     - javascript
     - Copy code

       ```javascript
       var fruits = ["apple", "banana", "orange"];
       ```
     - Object: Represents a collection of key-value pairs.
     - javascript
     - Copy code

- var person = { name: "Alice", age: 30, isStudent: false };
        - **Undefined:** Represents a variable that has been declared but not assigned a value.
        - javascript
        - Copy code
        - var x;
        - **Null:** Represents the absence of a value.
        - javascript
        - Copy code
        - var y = null;

3. **Variable Naming:**
    - Follows specific rules, including starting with a letter, underscore, or dollar sign.
    - Subsequent characters can include letters, numbers, underscores, or dollar signs.
    - Variables are case-sensitive.
    - javascript
    - Copy code
    - var firstName = "John"; var _counter = 0;

4. **Constants:**
    - Declared using the const keyword.
    - Cannot be reassigned after initialization.
    - javascript
    - Copy code
    - const PI = 3.14;

Understanding JavaScript variables and data types lays the foundation for creating dynamic and responsive web applications.

JavaScript Functions and Control

In JavaScript, functions and control structures are essential for creating dynamic and interactive web applications. Let's explore these concepts in detail:

Functions:

1. Function Declaration:
   - Functions are blocks of reusable code that perform a specific task.
   - Declared using the `function` keyword.
   - javascript
   - Copy code
   -
     ```javascript
     function greet(name) { console.log("Hello, " + name + "!");
     }
     ```

2. Function Invocation:
   - Functions are executed by invoking or calling them.
   - javascript
   - Copy code
   -
     ```javascript
     greet("Alice");
     ```

3. Parameters and Arguments:
   - Functions can have parameters (placeholders for values).
   - Arguments are the actual values passed to a function when it is called.
   - javascript
   - Copy code
   -
     ```javascript
     function add(a, b) { return a + b; } var sum = add(3, 5); // sum is now 8
     ```

4. Return Statement:
   - Functions can return a value using the `return` statement.
   - The function stops executing when a `return` statement is encountered.
   - javascript
   - Copy code

- o `function multiply(x, y) { return x * y; } var result = multiply(4, 6); // result is now 24`

Control Structures:

1. Conditional Statements:
   - o Control the flow of a program based on conditions.
   - o javascript
   - o Copy code
   - o `var age = 20; if (age >= 18) { console.log("You are an adult."); } else { console.log("You are a minor."); }`

2. Loops:
   - o Repeatedly execute a block of code until a certain condition is met.
   - o Common loops include `for`, `while`, and `do-while`.
   - o javascript
   - o Copy code
   - o `for (var i = 0; i < 5; i++) { console.log("Iteration " + i); }`

3. Switch Statement:
   - o Provides an alternative to multiple `if-else` statements based on the value of an expression.
   - o javascript
   - o Copy code
   - o `var day = "Monday"; switch (day) { case "Monday": console.log("It's the start of the week."); break; case "Friday": console.log("It's almost the weekend!"); break; default: console.log("It's a regular day."); }`

Understanding functions and control structures in JavaScript enables developers to create logic, handle user interactions, and build responsive applications.

JavaScript Objects and Arrays

In JavaScript, objects and arrays are powerful data structures that allow developers to organize and manipulate data in a structured way. Let's explore these concepts in detail:

Objects:

1. Object Definition:
    - Objects are collections of key-value pairs, where each key is a string (or Symbol) and each value can be any data type.
    - javascript
    - Copy code
    - var person = { name: "John", age: 30, isStudent: false };
2. Accessing Object Properties:
    - Properties of an object can be accessed using dot notation or bracket notation.
    - javascript
    - Copy code
    - var name = person.name; // Using dot notation var age = person["age"]; // Using bracket notation
3. Adding and Modifying Properties:
    - Properties can be added or modified after the object is created.
    - javascript
    - Copy code
    - person.gender = "Male"; // Adding a new property person.age = 31; // Modifying an existing property
4. Object Methods:
    - Objects can contain functions as values, known as methods.
    - javascript
    - Copy code

- ○ ```javascript
  var car = { brand: "Toyota", start: function() {
  console.log("Engine started."); } }; car.start(); //
  Invoking the method
  ```

Arrays:

1. Array Definition:
   - ○ Arrays are ordered lists of values, and each value can be of any data type.
   - ○ javascript
   - ○ Copy code
   - ○ ```javascript
     var fruits = ["apple", "banana", "orange"];
     ```

2. Accessing Array Elements:
   - ○ Elements of an array are accessed using zero-based indices.
   - ○ javascript
   - ○ Copy code
   - ○ ```javascript
     var firstFruit = fruits[0]; // Accessing the first element
     var secondFruit = fruits[1]; // Accessing the second element
     ```

3. Array Methods:
   - ○ Arrays come with built-in methods for common operations.
   - ○ javascript
   - ○ Copy code
   - ○ ```javascript
     fruits.push("grape"); // Adds an element to the end
     fruits.pop(); // Removes the last element
     ```

4. Nested Arrays and Objects:
   - ○ Arrays and objects can be nested within each other.
   - ○ javascript
   - ○ Copy code
   - ○ ```javascript
     var nestedData = [{ name: "John", age: 25 }, { name:
     "Alice", age: 30 }, ["apple", "banana", "orange"]];
     ```
     ```

Understanding how to work with objects and arrays in JavaScript is crucial for organizing and manipulating data effectively in web applications.

Linking HTML and CSS - Using External Style

In web development, linking HTML and CSS is a fundamental practice to apply styles and enhance the presentation of web pages. Using an external style sheet allows for better organization and maintainability of styles. Let's explore this process in detail:

External Style Sheet:

1. Create a CSS File:
   - Save your CSS styles in a separate file with a `.css` extension, for example, `styles.css`.
   - css
   - Copy code
   - ```css
     /* styles.css */ body { font-family: 'Arial', sans-serif; background-color: #f0f0f0; } h1 { color: #333; }
     ```

2. Link CSS in HTML:
   - In the HTML file, link the external CSS file within the `<head>` section using the `<link>` element.
   - html
   - Copy code
   - ```html
     <!-- index.html --> <!DOCTYPE html> <html lang="en"> <head> <meta charset="UTF-8"> <meta name="viewport" content="width=device-width, initial-scale=1.0"> <link rel="stylesheet" href="styles.css"> <title>Your Web Page</title> </head> <body> <!-- Your HTML content goes here --> <h1>Welcome to Your Web Page</h1> </body> </html>
     ```

3. Relative Path:
   - Ensure that the path specified in the `href` attribute of the `<link>` tag is relative to the location of your HTML file. If both files are in the same directory, a simple filename is sufficient. If they are in different directories, adjust the path accordingly.
4. Benefits of External Styles:
   - Separation of Concerns: Keeps HTML and CSS separate, making the codebase more modular and maintainable.
   - Reusability: Styles can be reused across multiple pages by linking the same external style sheet.
   - Consistency: Ensures a consistent look and feel across the website.

By linking HTML and CSS using an external style sheet, developers can efficiently manage styles, promote code reusability, and maintain a consistent design throughout their web projects.

Inline Styles and Embedded Style Sheets

In web development, HTML and CSS work together to structure and style web pages. Inline styles and embedded style sheets are methods of incorporating CSS directly within HTML. Let's explore these approaches in detail:

Inline Styles:
1. Usage in HTML Tags:
   - Apply styles directly within HTML tags using the `style` attribute.
   - html
   - Copy code
   - `<!-- index.html --> <!DOCTYPE html> <html lang="en"> <head> <meta charset="UTF-8"> <meta name="viewport"`

```
content="width=device-width, initial-scale=1.0"> <title>Your
Web Page</title> </head> <body> <h1 style="color: #333;
font-family: 'Arial', sans-serif;">Welcome to Your Web
Page</h1> </body> </html>
```

2. Benefits:
   - Quick application of styles for specific elements.
   - Useful for one-time or unique styling needs.
3. Drawbacks:
   - Reduced maintainability as styles are embedded within HTML.
   - Limited reusability across multiple elements or pages.

Embedded Style Sheets:
1. Usage in the `<style>` Tag:
   - Define styles within the `<style>` tag in the `<head>` section of the HTML file.
   - html
   - Copy code
   -
```
<!-- index.html --> <!DOCTYPE html> <html lang="en"> <head>
<meta charset="UTF-8"> <meta name="viewport"
content="width=device-width, initial-scale=1.0"> <title>Your
Web Page</title> <style> body { font-family: 'Arial', sans-
serif; background-color: #f0f0f0; } h1 { color: #333; }
</style> </head> <body> <h1>Welcome to Your Web Page</h1>
</body> </html>
```

2. Benefits:
   - Improved maintainability compared to inline styles.
   - Styles can be applied to multiple elements within the same document.
3. Drawbacks:
   - Styles are still embedded within the HTML file.

- Limited reusability across different HTML files.

Using inline styles and embedded style sheets provides flexibility in applying styles directly within HTML. However, for larger projects or enhanced maintainability, linking an external style sheet is often preferred.

Creating Dynamic Web Pages with JavaScript - Document Object Model (DOM)

JavaScript plays a crucial role in making web pages interactive and dynamic. The Document Object Model (DOM) is a programming interface that represents the structure of an HTML document as a tree-like structure. This allows developers to manipulate the content, structure, and style of a web page dynamically.

Document Object Model (DOM) Overview:

1. Representation of HTML Structure:
   - The DOM represents an HTML document as a tree structure, where each HTML element is a node in the tree.
   - The root of the tree is the `document` object, which corresponds to the entire HTML document.
2. Nodes and Elements:
   - HTML elements, attributes, and text content are represented as nodes in the DOM.
   - Elements are the structural components like `<div>`, `<p>`, or `<h1>`.
   - Attributes and text content are also nodes in the DOM.
3. Hierarchy and Relationships:
   - The DOM establishes parent-child relationships between nodes based on the HTML structure.

- o Nodes can be accessed, traversed, and manipulated using JavaScript.

4. Dynamic Manipulation:
   - o JavaScript allows developers to dynamically update, modify, or create new content on a web page.
   - o Changes made to the DOM automatically reflect in the displayed content without requiring a page refresh.

JavaScript and DOM Interaction:

1. Accessing Elements:
   - o Elements can be accessed using various methods like `getElementById`, `getElementsByClassName`, `getElementsByTagName`, or more modern methods like `querySelector` and `querySelectorAll`.
2. Modifying Content:
   - o Content can be changed by updating the `innerHTML` or `textContent` properties of an element.
   - o Attributes can be modified using methods like `setAttribute` and `removeAttribute`.
3. Manipulating Styles:
   - o Styles can be dynamically applied or removed using the `style` property.
   - o CSS classes can be added or removed to change the styling dynamically.
4. Handling Events:
   - o JavaScript allows the attachment of event listeners to respond to user interactions (e.g., clicks, keypresses).
   - o Event listeners trigger functions that handle the specified events.

Benefits of DOM Manipulation:

1. Dynamic User Experience:
   - Enables the creation of interactive and responsive web pages.
2. Real-Time Updates:
   - Allows for real-time updates without requiring a full page reload.
3. Enhanced Interactivity:
   - Enables developers to respond to user actions and create dynamic interfaces.

Understanding the Document Object Model is essential for harnessing the full power of JavaScript in creating engaging and dynamic web pages.

Events and Event Handling

In web development, events are occurrences or interactions on a web page that can trigger specific JavaScript functionality. Event handling involves capturing and responding to these events, allowing developers to create interactive and dynamic web pages.

Events in JavaScript:
1. Common Events:
   - Events can be user-triggered, such as clicks, keypresses, mouse movements, or form submissions.
   - Other events include page loading, resizing, or focus changes.
2. Event Listeners:
   - Event listeners are functions that "listen" for a specific event to occur.
   - They are attached to HTML elements and execute a designated function when the associated event occurs.

Event Handling in JavaScript:

1. Attaching Event Listeners:
   - Use the `addEventListener` method to attach an event listener to an HTML element.
   - Specify the event type and the function to be executed when the event occurs.
   - javascript
   - Copy code

```javascript
// Example: Attaching a click event listener to a button var
button = document.getElementById('myButton');
button.addEventListener('click', handleClick);
```

2. Event Object:
   - When an event occurs, an event object is created.
   - This object contains information about the event, such as the target element, type of event, and additional data.
   - javascript
   - Copy code

```javascript
function handleClick(event) { console.log('Button clicked!',
event.target); }
```

3. Preventing Default Behavior:
   - Some events, like form submissions or link clicks, have default behaviors.
   - Use `event.preventDefault()` to prevent the default action from taking place.
   - javascript
   - Copy code

```javascript
document.getElementById('myForm') addEventListener('submit',
function(event) { event.preventDefault(); // Custom form
submission handling });
```

4. Event Bubbling and Capturing:

- Events propagate through the DOM tree in two phases: capturing and bubbling.
- Use the `addEventListener` method's third parameter to control the event flow.
- javascript
- Copy code

```javascript
// Example: Adding an event listener with capturing
element.addEventListener('click', handleClick, true);
```

5. Event Delegation:

- Rather than attaching event listeners to individual elements, use event delegation to handle events for multiple elements with a common ancestor.
- javascript
- Copy code

```javascript
document.getElementById('parentContainer').addEventListener('click', function(event) { if (event.target.tagName === 'BUTTON') { // Handle button click } });
```

Benefits of Event Handling:

1. Interactivity:
   - Enables developers to respond to user actions, creating interactive web experiences.
2. Asynchronous Behavior:
   - Allows for asynchronous programming, responding to events independently of the main program flow.
3. Dynamic Updates:
   - Dynamically update content or styles in response to user interactions.

Understanding events and event handling is crucial for building responsive and user-friendly web applications with JavaScript.

Responsive Web Development - Flexible Layouts and Media Queries

Responsive web development involves designing and building websites that adapt and look good on various devices and screen sizes. Two key aspects of achieving responsiveness are flexible layouts and media queries.

Flexible Layouts:

1. Fluid Grids:
    - Use relative units like percentages for widths and heights rather than fixed pixels.
    - Create fluid grids that scale with the viewport size.
    - css
    - Copy code
    - ```
      .container { width: 90%; margin: 0 auto; /* Center the
      container */ } .column { width: 30%; /* Example: Three
      columns in a row */ float: left; }
      ```

2. Flexible Images:
    - Ensure images scale proportionally within their containers.
    - Set the maximum width of images to 100% to prevent overflow.
    - css
    - Copy code
    - ```
      img { max-width: 100%; height: auto; }
      ```

3. Media Queries:
    - Media queries are conditional statements in CSS that apply styles based on the characteristics of the device or viewport.

- o Use media queries to define breakpoints where styles should change.
- o css
- o Copy code
- o /* Example: Change styles when the viewport width is 600 pixels or less */ @media only screen and (max-width: 600px) { .column { width: 100%; /* Full width for small screens */ } }

Media Queries:

1. Viewport Sizes:
   - o Media queries can target specific viewport sizes using min-width and max-width.
   - o css
   - o Copy code
   - o @media only screen and (min-width: 768px) and (max-width: 1024px) { /* Styles for tablets */ }

2. Device Types:
   - o Apply styles based on the type of device, such as screen, print, or handheld.
   - o css
   - o Copy code
   - o @media only print { /* Styles for print */ }

3. Orientation:
   - o Adjust styles based on the orientation of the device (landscape or portrait).
   - o css
   - o Copy code
   - o @media only screen and (orientation: landscape) { /* Styles for landscape orientation */ }

4. Combining Conditions:

- Combine multiple conditions in media queries for precise targeting.
- css
- Copy code
- @media only screen and (min-width: 600px) and (orientation: landscape) { /* Styles for landscape orientation on screens wider than 600 pixels */ }

Benefits of Responsive Design:

1. Improved User Experience:
   - Ensures a consistent and optimal viewing experience across different devices.
2. SEO Benefits:
   - Google favors mobile-friendly websites in search rankings.
3. Cost-Effective:
   - Eliminates the need for separate websites or apps for different devices.

Implementing flexible layouts and media queries is essential for creating websites that adapt seamlessly to the diverse landscape of devices and screen sizes.

Mobile-Friendly Design Practices

Mobile-friendly design practices are essential in responsive web development to ensure optimal user experiences on various mobile devices. Implementing these practices involves considering the unique challenges and characteristics of smaller screens and touch interfaces.

Touch-Friendly Navigation:

1. Larger Tap Targets:

- o Increase the size of interactive elements like buttons and links to make them easier to tap.
- o css
- o Copy code
- o

```
/* Example: Increase button size for better touch
interaction */ button { padding: 15px; font-size: 16px; }
```

2. Avoid Hover-Dependent Actions:
   - o Since mobile devices don't have hover states, avoid relying on hover-dependent actions for crucial functionality.

Optimized Content:

1. Condensed Content:
   - o Streamline content for smaller screens, prioritizing essential information.
   - o Use collapsible menus or accordions to manage content hierarchy.
   - o css
   - o Copy code
   - o

```
/* Example: Hide secondary content on small screens */
.secondary-content { display: none; } @media only screen and
(max-width: 600px) { .secondary-content { display: block; }
}
```

2. Optimized Images:
   - o Use responsive images and implement image compression techniques to reduce load times.
   - o Set image dimensions to ensure proper scaling on different devices.

Adaptive Typography:

1. Relative Font Sizes:

- Use relative units like `em` or `rem` for font sizes to ensure text remains readable across various screen sizes.
  - css
  - Copy code
  - `/* Example: Set font size relative to the base font size */ body { font-size: 16px; } h1 { font-size: 2em; /* 32px on a 16px base font size */ }`

2. Line Height:
   - Adjust line height for improved readability on smaller screens.

Viewport Meta Tag:

1. Viewport Configuration:
   - Use the viewport meta tag to configure the viewport's initial scale and dimensions.
2. html
3. Copy code
4. `<!-- Example: Set initial scale and enable user scaling --> <meta name="viewport" content="width=device-width, initial-scale=1, user-scalable=yes">`

Testing and Debugging:

1. Cross-Browser Testing:
   - Test your website across various mobile browsers to ensure consistent performance.
2. Device Emulators:
   - Use browser developer tools or dedicated emulators to simulate different devices.

Benefits of Mobile-Friendly Design:

1. Enhanced User Engagement:

   o Users are more likely to engage with and navigate mobile-friendly
     websites.

2. Improved SEO:

   o Google prioritizes mobile-friendly websites in search rankings.

3. Wider Accessibility:

   o Ensures accessibility for users on a broad range of devices.

By incorporating mobile-friendly design practices, developers can create web
experiences that cater to the diverse landscape of mobile devices, enhancing
usability and accessibility.

Introduction to Web Projects

Planning and Developing Web Applications

Successfully planning and developing web applications requires a structured and
comprehensive approach. This involves careful consideration of project
requirements, user needs, and effective collaboration among development teams.
Here's an exploration of key aspects in planning and developing web applications.

Project Planning:

1. Understanding Requirements:

   o Begin by thoroughly understanding the project requirements, including
     functionality, user expectations, and business goals.

   o Engage with stakeholders to gather insights and create a detailed
     project scope.

2. Defining Goals and Objectives:

- Clearly define the goals and objectives of the web application. What purpose will it serve, and what outcomes are expected?
3. Target Audience Analysis:
    - Identify the target audience and their needs. Consider user personas to tailor the application to the intended users.
4. Technology Stack Selection:
    - Choose an appropriate technology stack based on project requirements. This includes selecting programming languages, frameworks, and databases.

Development Process:
1. Agile Development Methodology:
    - Adopt an agile development methodology to facilitate iterative development and continuous feedback.
    - Break down the project into sprints, each delivering a set of features.
2. Wireframing and Prototyping:
    - Create wireframes and prototypes to visualize the application's layout and user flow.
    - This helps in early visualization and feedback collection.
3. Responsive Design:
    - Prioritize responsive design to ensure the application is accessible and functional across various devices and screen sizes.
4. Collaboration and Version Control:
    - Use version control systems like Git to manage code changes and collaborate effectively among team members.
    - Platforms like GitHub or GitLab provide centralized repositories and collaboration tools.
5. Testing and Quality Assurance:

- Implement a robust testing strategy, including unit testing, integration testing, and end-to-end testing.
- Prioritize quality assurance to identify and address bugs and issues promptly.

Documentation:

1. Code Documentation:
   - Maintain thorough documentation for the codebase to assist developers and ensure code readability.
   - Include comments, explanations of complex logic, and documentation for APIs.
2. User Documentation:
   - Provide user documentation to guide end-users on how to navigate and use the web application effectively.

Deployment and Maintenance:

1. Deployment Strategy:
   - Plan a deployment strategy that ensures a smooth transition from development to production.
   - Consider continuous integration and continuous deployment (CI/CD) practices for automated and streamlined deployments.
2. Monitoring and Updates:
   - Implement monitoring tools to track application performance and detect issues.
   - Regularly update the application to introduce new features, enhancements, and security patches.

Benefits of Comprehensive Planning:

1. Efficient Development Process:
   - Well-planned projects are more likely to proceed smoothly and efficiently, minimizing delays and disruptions.
2. Reduced Risks:
   - Identifying potential challenges and risks during the planning phase allows for proactive mitigation strategies.
3. Client and User Satisfaction:
   - Clear goals and well-defined requirements lead to more satisfactory outcomes for clients and end-users.

By approaching web projects with a thoughtful planning phase and following best development practices, teams can create robust and successful web applications that meet both client expectations and user needs.

Basics of Version Control

Version control is a crucial aspect of web development, providing a systematic way to manage and track changes in code throughout the development lifecycle. This process ensures collaboration among team members, helps in identifying and resolving issues, and maintains a historical record of code changes. Let's delve into the basics of version control in the context of web projects.

Key Concepts:
1. Repository:
   - A repository (or repo) is a centralized location where the project's source code and its history are stored.
   - Repositories can be local (on a developer's machine) or remote (hosted on platforms like GitHub, GitLab, or Bitbucket).
2. Commit:

- A commit is a snapshot of the project at a specific point in time. It includes changes to files, additions, deletions, or modifications.
- Commits are accompanied by commit messages that describe the changes made.

3. Branch:
   - Branches are independent lines of development within a repository. They allow developers to work on features or fixes without affecting the main codebase.
   - Branches can be created, merged, or deleted as needed.

Common Version Control Systems:

1. Git:
   - Git is a distributed version control system widely used in web development.
   - It allows multiple developers to work on the same project simultaneously and independently.

2. GitHub, GitLab, Bitbucket:
   - These platforms host remote repositories and provide collaboration features.
   - Developers can clone repositories, create branches, submit pull requests, and manage issues.

Basic Workflow:

1. Initializing a Repository:
   - To start version control, developers initialize a repository either locally or on a remote platform.

2. Cloning a Repository:

- Developers can clone an existing repository to their local machine, creating a copy of the project's codebase.

3. Creating Branches:
   - Developers create branches to work on specific features or bug fixes without affecting the main codebase.

4. Making Commits:
   - As changes are made to the code, developers make commits to document and save those changes.

5. Merging:
   - Once a feature or fix is complete and tested, developers merge their branches back into the main branch.

6. Pull Requests:
   - On platforms like GitHub, developers can submit pull requests to propose changes to the main codebase.
   - Code reviews and discussions often occur within pull requests before merging.

Benefits of Version Control:

1. Collaboration:
   - Enables multiple developers to work on the same project concurrently while maintaining code integrity.

2. History Tracking:
   - Maintains a detailed history of code changes, making it easier to understand and revert to previous states if needed.

3. Branching Strategies:
   - Facilitates the implementation of branching strategies for parallel development and feature isolation.

4. Error Identification:

- Aids in identifying when and where errors were introduced, simplifying debugging.
5. Team Coordination:
- Promotes effective collaboration by providing a shared platform for code sharing and reviews.

Understanding the basics of version control is fundamental for modern web development practices, fostering collaboration, code stability, and project traceability.

Additional Topics

Fundamentals of Web Security

Ensuring web security is paramount in web development to safeguard sensitive information, protect user privacy, and prevent unauthorized access. The fundamentals of web security involve implementing robust measures to mitigate potential vulnerabilities and threats. Let's explore key aspects of web security.

Encryption:
1. SSL/TLS (Secure Socket Layer/Transport Layer Security):
- Implement SSL/TLS protocols to encrypt data transmitted between a user's browser and the web server.
- This ensures that sensitive information, such as login credentials and personal data, remains confidential.

Authentication and Authorization:

1. Strong Password Policies:
   - Enforce strong password requirements to enhance user account security.
   - Encourage the use of complex passwords with a combination of letters, numbers, and special characters.
2. Multi-Factor Authentication (MFA):
   - Implement MFA to add an extra layer of security beyond passwords.
   - This typically involves using a secondary authentication method, such as a code sent to a user's mobile device.
3. Role-Based Access Control (RBAC):
   - Employ RBAC to restrict access based on user roles and responsibilities.
   - Users should only have access to the information and functionalities necessary for their roles.

Cross-Site Scripting (XSS) Prevention:
1. Input Validation:
   - Validate and sanitize user inputs to prevent malicious code injection.
   - Use server-side validation to ensure that data received from users is safe and adheres to expected formats.
2. Content Security Policy (CSP):
   - Implement CSP headers to define and control the sources from which certain types of content can be loaded.
   - This helps prevent the execution of malicious scripts.

Cross-Site Request Forgery (CSRF) Protection:
1. Anti-CSRF Tokens:

- Include anti-CSRF tokens in forms to validate that the form submission originated from the legitimate user.
- This helps prevent attackers from forcing users to perform actions unintentionally.

Security Headers:

1. HTTP Security Headers:
   - Set HTTP security headers, such as `Strict-Transport-Security` and `X-Content-Type-Options`, to enhance security.
   - These headers instruct browsers on how to handle aspects like content types and secure connections.

Regular Security Audits:

1. Vulnerability Scanning:
   - Regularly perform vulnerability scanning to identify and address potential security weaknesses.
   - Automated tools can help detect vulnerabilities in code and configurations.
2. Penetration Testing:
   - Conduct penetration testing to simulate real-world attacks and identify vulnerabilities that might not be apparent through automated scans.
   - This involves ethical hacking to assess the system's security posture.

Logging and Monitoring:

1. Security Logging:
   - Implement comprehensive logging of security-relevant events.
   - Regularly review logs to detect and respond to potential security incidents.

2. Intrusion Detection Systems (IDS):

    o   Deploy IDS to monitor network and system activities for signs of
        unauthorized access or malicious behavior.

Regular Software Updates:

1. Patch Management:

    o   Keep all software, including web servers, frameworks, and libraries, up
        to date with the latest security patches.

    o   Regularly check for updates and apply them promptly.

Implementing these fundamental web security practices is crucial for creating a
robust defense against potential threats and ensuring a secure environment for both
users and data.

Performance Optimization

Achieving optimal performance is crucial for delivering a seamless and efficient user
experience in web development. Performance optimization involves implementing
strategies to enhance website speed, responsiveness, and overall efficiency. Let's
explore key aspects of performance optimization.

Code Efficiency:

1. Minification and Compression:

    o   Minify CSS, JavaScript, and HTML files to reduce their size and
        decrease load times.

    o   Implement compression techniques (gzip or Brotli) to further reduce file
        sizes during transmission.

2. Optimized Images:

- o Compress and resize images to an appropriate resolution without compromising quality.
  - o Consider using modern image formats like WebP for better compression.
3. Lazy Loading:
  - o Implement lazy loading for images and other non-essential resources.
  - o Load resources only when they are needed, improving initial page load times.

Caching Strategies:

1. Browser Caching:
  - o Leverage browser caching to store static resources locally on users' devices.
  - o Set appropriate cache headers to control how long browsers should cache assets.
2. CDN (Content Delivery Network):
  - o Use a CDN to distribute static content across multiple servers geographically closer to users.
  - o This reduces latency and accelerates content delivery.

Efficient Server-Side Practices:

1. Server-Side Caching:
  - o Implement server-side caching mechanisms to store frequently accessed data.
  - o Reduce the need to regenerate content for each user request.
2. Database Optimization:
  - o Optimize database queries and indexes to enhance database performance.

- o Use database connection pooling to manage and reuse database connections efficiently.

Front-End Performance:

1. Asynchronous Loading:
   - o Load scripts asynchronously to prevent them from blocking the rendering of the page.
   - o Place non-essential scripts at the end of the HTML document or use the `async` attribute.
2. CSS and JavaScript Bundling:
   - o Bundle multiple CSS and JavaScript files into a single file to reduce the number of HTTP requests.
   - o This minimizes loading times by fetching fewer resources.

Monitoring and Analytics:

1. Performance Monitoring:
   - o Utilize performance monitoring tools to identify bottlenecks and areas for improvement.
   - o Monitor metrics such as page load time, server response time, and resource utilization.
2. User Analytics:
   - o Analyze user behavior and interactions to understand how users engage with the website.
   - o Use this data to optimize the most critical user pathways.

Progressive Web App (PWA) Features:

1. Service Workers:

- Implement service workers to enable offline capabilities and faster loading on repeat visits.
- Service workers cache resources, allowing the application to function offline or in low-network conditions.

Responsive Design:

1. Media Queries:
   - Use responsive design principles and media queries to adapt layouts to different screen sizes.
   - Optimize styles and layouts for mobile devices, tablets, and desktops.

Benefits of Performance Optimization:

1. Enhanced User Experience:
   - Faster load times contribute to a positive user experience and higher user satisfaction.
2. Improved SEO:
   - Search engines prioritize faster-loading websites, positively impacting search rankings.
3. Reduced Bounce Rates:
   - Optimal performance reduces bounce rates as users are more likely to stay and engage with the content.

By implementing these performance optimization strategies, web developers can create websites that load quickly, respond efficiently, and provide an overall improved experience for users.

Practical Projects

Building a Simple Webpage

Building a simple webpage is an excellent starting point for individuals learning web development. This practical project involves creating a basic webpage using HTML and CSS to understand the fundamentals of structure, styling, and layout. Let's break down the steps involved in building a simple webpage.

1. **Project Setup:**
   - Create a new project folder on your computer to organize your files.
   - Inside the project folder, create two files: `index.html` for the HTML structure and `styles.css` for the CSS styles.

2. **HTML Structure (index.html):**
   - Define the basic structure of your HTML file.
   - Include the following elements:
   - html
   - Copy code
   - ```
     <!DOCTYPE html> <html lang="en"> <head> <meta charset="UTF-8">
     <meta name="viewport" content="width=device-width, initial-
     scale=1.0"> <link rel="stylesheet" href="styles.css"> <title>Your
     Webpage Title</title> </head> <body> <!-- Your webpage content
     goes here --> </body> </html>
     ```

3. **Content Section:**
   - Inside the `<body>` tag, add content to your webpage.
   - Include headings, paragraphs, images, or any other elements you want to display.
   - For example:
   - html
   - Copy code
     ```

- `<h1>Welcome to My Simple Webpage</h1> <p>This is a basic webpage created for learning web development.</p> <img src="your-image.jpg" alt="Description of your image">`

4. CSS Styling (styles.css):

- Link the CSS file to your HTML file using the `<link>` tag in the `<head>` section.
- Define styles in your `styles.css` file to enhance the visual presentation.
- For example:
- css
- Copy code
- `body { font-family: 'Arial', sans-serif; background-color: #f0f0f0; color: #333; text-align: center; padding: 20px; } h1 { color: #008080; } img { max-width: 100%; height: auto; margin-top: 20px; }`

5. Testing and Refining:

- Open your `index.html` file in a web browser to see your webpage.
- Make adjustments to the HTML and CSS as needed.
- Test the responsiveness by resizing the browser window.

6. Expand and Customize:

- Experiment by adding more content and styling to your webpage.
- Explore additional HTML tags and CSS properties to enhance your skills.
- Consider creating multiple pages and interlinking them.

7. Validation and Accessibility:

- Validate your HTML and CSS code using online validators to ensure correctness.

- Ensure accessibility by using appropriate alt attributes for images and maintaining a logical document structure.

8. **Version Control:**
   - Consider initializing a version control system (e.g., Git) to track changes and collaborate with others.

9. **Deployment:**
   - If you have a hosting service, deploy your simple webpage to share it with others.
   - Alternatively, use platforms like GitHub Pages for free hosting.

Building a simple webpage provides hands-on experience with essential web development concepts and serves as a foundation for more complex projects. As you progress, explore additional technologies and frameworks to enhance your skills further.

Developing an Interactive Application

Embarking on the development of an interactive application is a rewarding project that allows you to delve deeper into web development, incorporating JavaScript for dynamic functionality. Here's a breakdown of the steps involved in developing an interactive application.

1. **Define Project Scope:**
   - Clearly outline the purpose and features of your interactive application.
   - Identify the target audience and the problem your application aims to solve or the experience it provides.

2. **Set Up Project Structure:**

- Create a new project folder with organized subdirectories for HTML, CSS, and JavaScript files.
- Consider using a modern project structure or utilizing a framework like React, Angular, or Vue for more complex applications.

3. **HTML Structure (index.html):**

- Design the HTML structure, incorporating containers for different sections of your application.
- Include placeholders for dynamic content and user interactions.

4. **CSS Styling (styles.css):**

- Develop styles to create an appealing and responsive layout for your application.
- Ensure a consistent design that aligns with the overall user experience.

5. **JavaScript Interactivity (script.js):**

- Implement JavaScript functionality to make your application interactive.
- Handle user inputs, create dynamic content, and manage application state.
- Utilize event listeners for user interactions such as clicks, form submissions, or key presses.

6. **API Integration (Optional):**

- If applicable, integrate external APIs to fetch data and enhance the functionality of your application.
- Handle API requests and responses in your JavaScript code.

7. **Testing and Debugging:**

- Regularly test your application in different browsers to ensure cross-browser compatibility.
- Use developer tools for debugging and addressing any issues that arise during testing.

8. User Feedback and Notifications:
- Implement feedback mechanisms to inform users about the success or failure of their actions.
- Utilize alerts, notifications, or visual cues to enhance the user experience.

9. Responsive Design:
- Ensure your application is responsive and accessible on various devices and screen sizes.
- Test responsiveness by resizing the browser window and using different devices.

10. Security Considerations:
- Implement secure coding practices to protect against common vulnerabilities.
- Sanitize user inputs and validate data to prevent potential security risks.

11. Documentation:
- Document your code, especially if the project is intended for collaboration or future reference.
- Include clear comments and instructions for developers who might work on the project.

12. User Testing:

- Conduct user testing to gather feedback on the usability and effectiveness of your application.
- Make iterative improvements based on user feedback.

13. **Deployment:**
   - Choose a hosting solution to deploy your interactive application.
   - Platforms like Netlify, Vercel, or GitHub Pages offer straightforward deployment options.

14. **Continuous Improvement:**
   - Consider incorporating user feedback and analytics to make ongoing improvements.
   - Explore additional features or optimizations based on user needs and technological advancements.

Developing an interactive application is an exciting journey that allows you to apply a comprehensive set of skills in web development. By following these steps, you can create a user-friendly and engaging application that showcases your proficiency in HTML, CSS, and JavaScript.

References and Resources

Recommended Literature

Exploring additional literature is essential for deepening your understanding of web development. The following list comprises recommended readings to enhance your knowledge and skills in HTML, CSS, and JavaScript, as well as broader web development topics.

1. **HTML and CSS: Design and Build Websites (Jon Duckett)**
   - A visually engaging book that covers the fundamentals of HTML and CSS. Suitable for beginners and those looking to strengthen their foundation.

2. **JavaScript: The Good Parts (Douglas Crockford)**
   - Douglas Crockford explores the good parts of JavaScript, offering valuable insights into the language's strengths and best practices.

3. **Eloquent JavaScript (Marijn Haverbeke)**
   - An in-depth guide to JavaScript, covering topics from basic syntax to advanced concepts. Ideal for individuals looking to deepen their JavaScript knowledge.

4. **You Don't Know JS (Kyle Simpson)**
   - A series of books diving into the intricate details of JavaScript. It provides a comprehensive understanding of the language for developers at different skill levels.

5. **CSS Secrets: Better Solutions to Everyday Web Design Problems (Lea Verou)**
   - Lea Verou shares creative CSS solutions to common design challenges, offering practical tips and techniques for more efficient styling.

6. **JavaScript: The Definitive Guide (David Flanagan)**
   - A comprehensive reference guide for JavaScript, suitable for both beginners and experienced developers. It covers the language in-depth and includes practical examples.

7. **Responsive Web Design (Ethan Marcotte)**
   - Ethan Marcotte introduces the concept of responsive web design, providing techniques and best practices for creating websites that adapt to various screen sizes.

8. **Clean Code: A Handbook of Agile Software Craftsmanship (Robert C. Martin)**
   - While not specific to web development, this book emphasizes writing clean, maintainable code, which is crucial for any software development endeavor.

9. **The Pragmatic Programmer: Your Journey to Mastery (Dave Thomas, Andy Hunt)**
   - A classic guide covering various aspects of software development, offering practical advice and timeless principles for becoming a proficient programmer.

10. **MDN Web Docs (Mozilla Developer Network)**
    - An online resource offering comprehensive documentation on HTML, CSS, JavaScript, and web development technologies. It serves as a valuable reference throughout your learning journey.

Remember to explore online platforms, forums, and community discussions to stay updated on the latest trends and advancements in web development. Continuous learning and practical application are key to mastering the ever-evolving field of web development.

Online Sources and Communities

Accessing online sources and engaging with web development communities is crucial for staying updated on industry trends, sharing experiences, and seeking support. The following list highlights recommended online sources and communities for web developers:

1. MDN Web Docs

- The Mozilla Developer Network offers extensive documentation on HTML, CSS, JavaScript, and web technologies. It serves as a reliable reference for developers of all skill levels.

2. W3Schools

- W3Schools provides comprehensive tutorials and references on web development technologies. It's an excellent resource for learning and quick reference.

3. Stack Overflow

- A vibrant community where developers ask and answer technical questions. Stack Overflow is an invaluable resource for troubleshooting and seeking guidance on coding challenges.

4. GitHub

- GitHub is a platform for version control and collaborative development. Explore repositories, contribute to open-source projects, and learn from others' code.

5. Dev.to

- Dev.to is a community-driven platform where developers share articles, tutorials, and discussions. It's a supportive space for learning and networking.

6. CSS-Tricks

- CSS-Tricks provides tutorials, articles, and tips specifically focused on CSS. It's a valuable resource for mastering styling techniques.

7. Smashing Magazine

- Smashing Magazine offers articles and resources on web design and development. It covers a broad range of topics, including best practices and industry trends.

8. FreeCodeCamp

- FreeCodeCamp provides a structured curriculum for learning web development. It includes interactive challenges and projects to reinforce your skills.

9. CodePen

- CodePen is a social development environment for front-end developers. Explore, share, and showcase your HTML, CSS, and JavaScript creations.

10. Reddit - r/webdev

- The web development subreddit is a community where developers discuss industry news, share insights, and seek advice. It's a great platform for connecting with fellow developers.

11. WebPlatform.org

- WebPlatform.org offers documentation, guides, and resources for web developers. It focuses on creating a comprehensive and up-to-date reference.

12. CSS Tricks Discord

- Joining the CSS Tricks Discord community allows real-time discussions, collaboration, and networking with other developers.

13. Mozilla Developer

- Mozilla Developer's learning area provides hands-on tutorials and projects for mastering web technologies.

Engaging with these online sources and communities will enhance your learning experience, provide valuable insights, and connect you with a global network of web developers. Regular participation in discussions and staying curious about emerging technologies will contribute to your continuous growth in the field.

We hope this book will guide you through the exploration of the HTML, CSS, and JavaScript world!